HOW
TO
SUCCEED
WITH
WOMEN
WITHOUT
REALLY
TRYING

THE ART OF SUCCEEDING

Text by
SHEPHERD MEAD

Illustrations by
Claude Smith

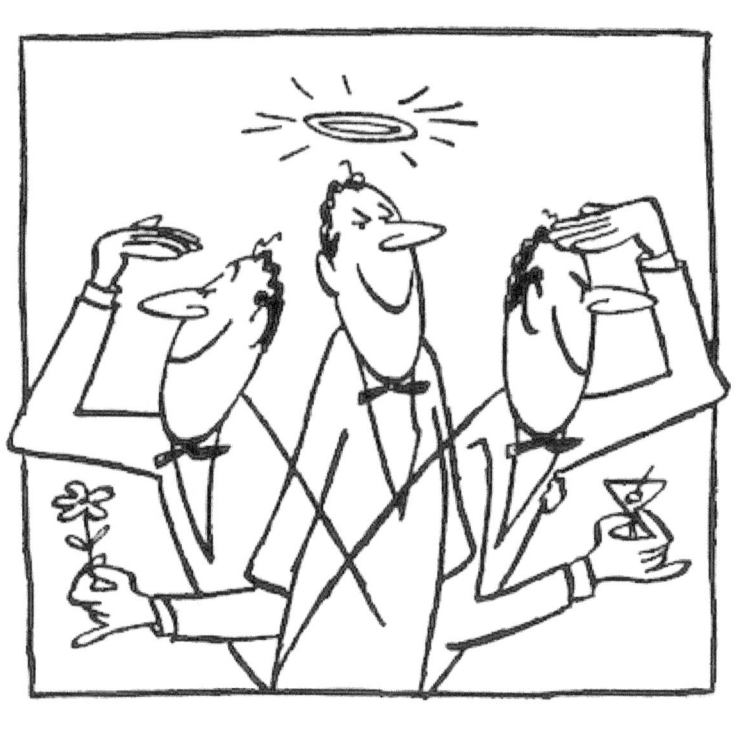

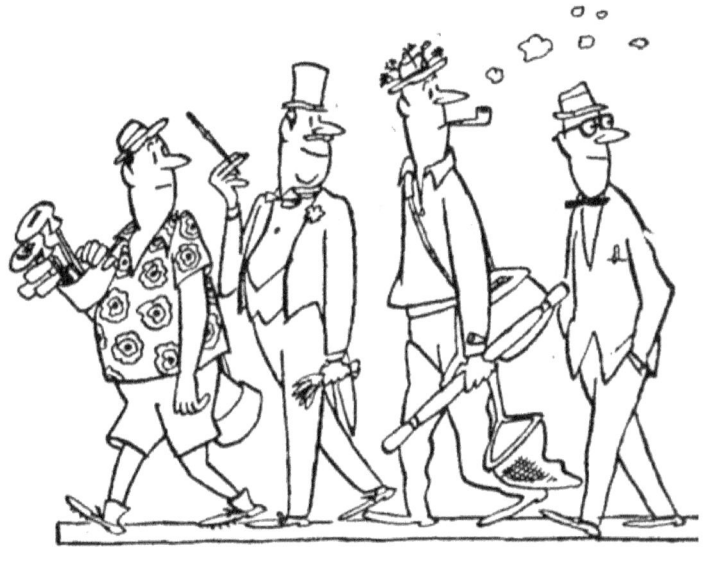

Without the real power of reproduction

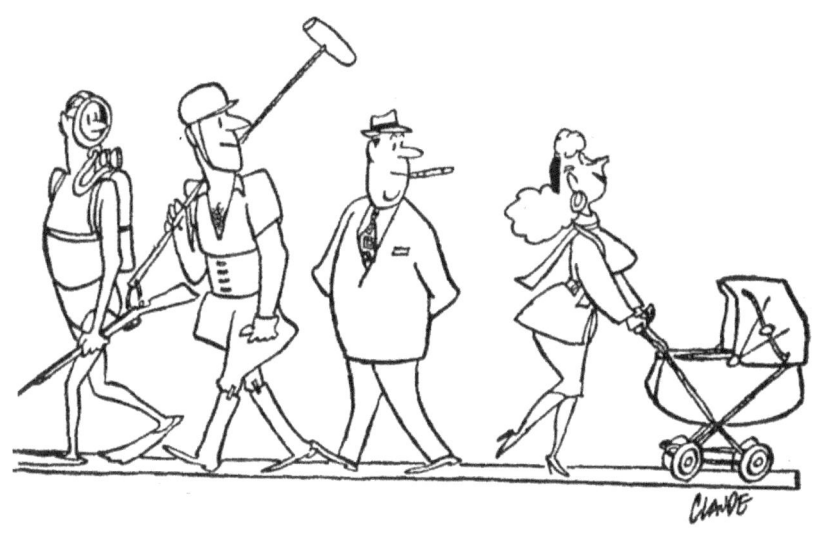

...or the solace of motherhood.

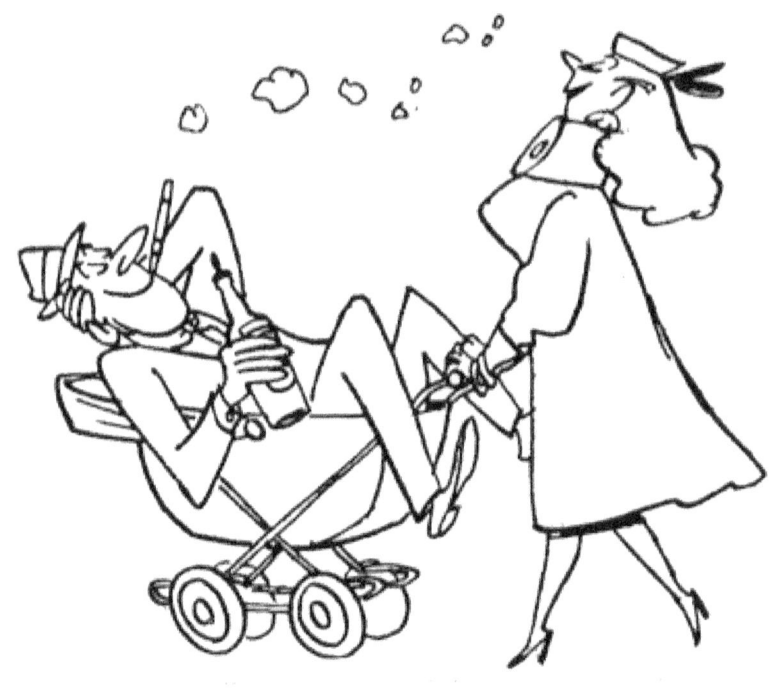

Women prefer tall men and small boys—and are happiest of all when they find a male who is both at the same time.

An embarrassed father is a poor companion.

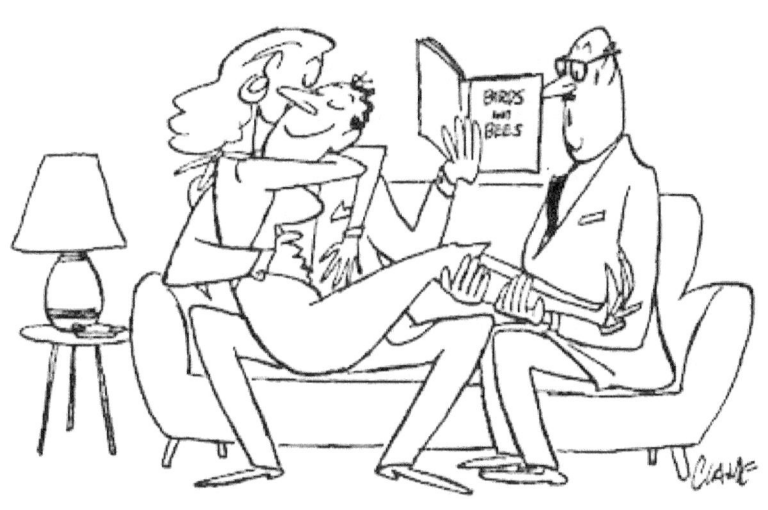

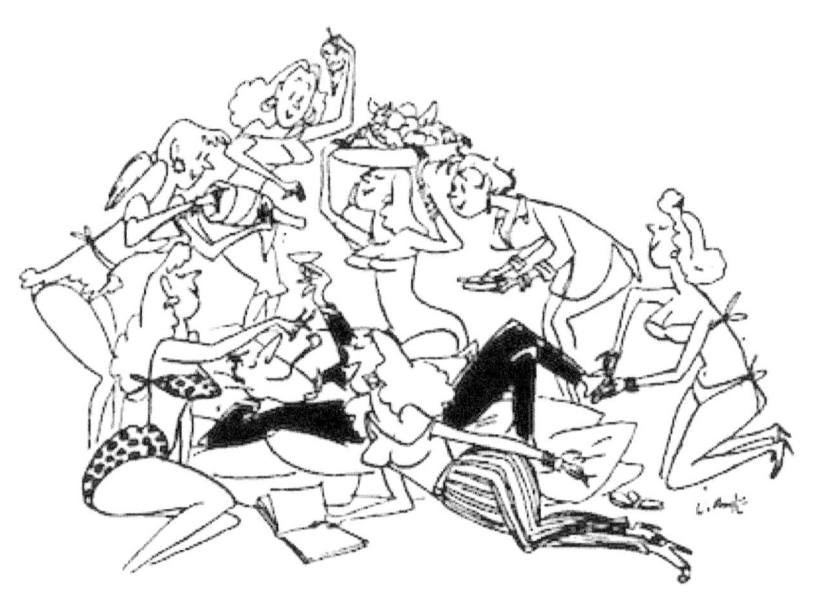

The bachelor can be surrounded
by girls of all kinds.

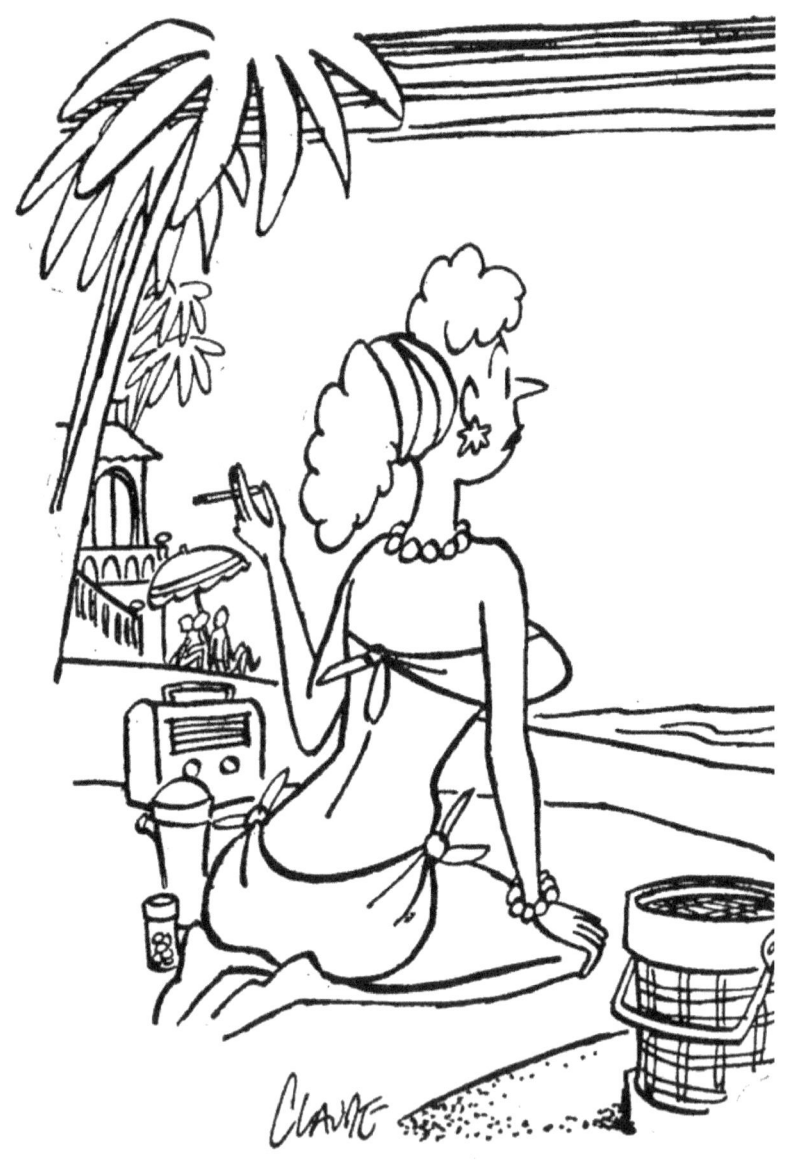

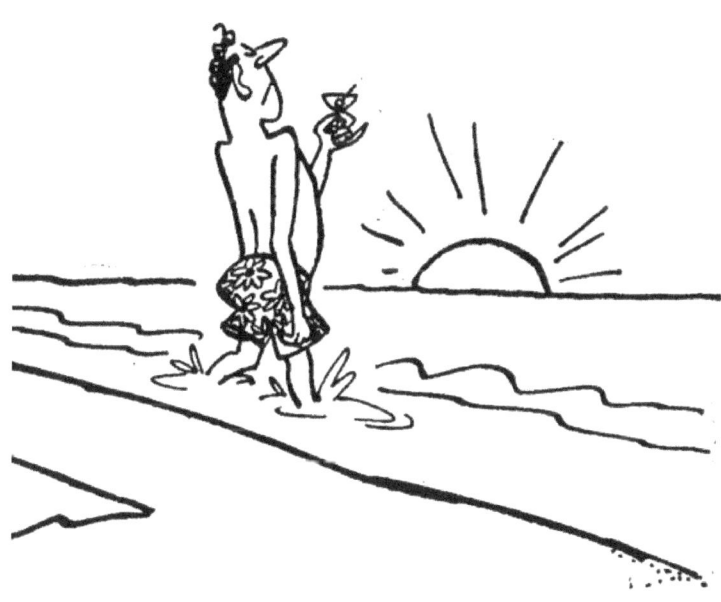

"C'est la vie."

Do your best to paint them a rosy picture.

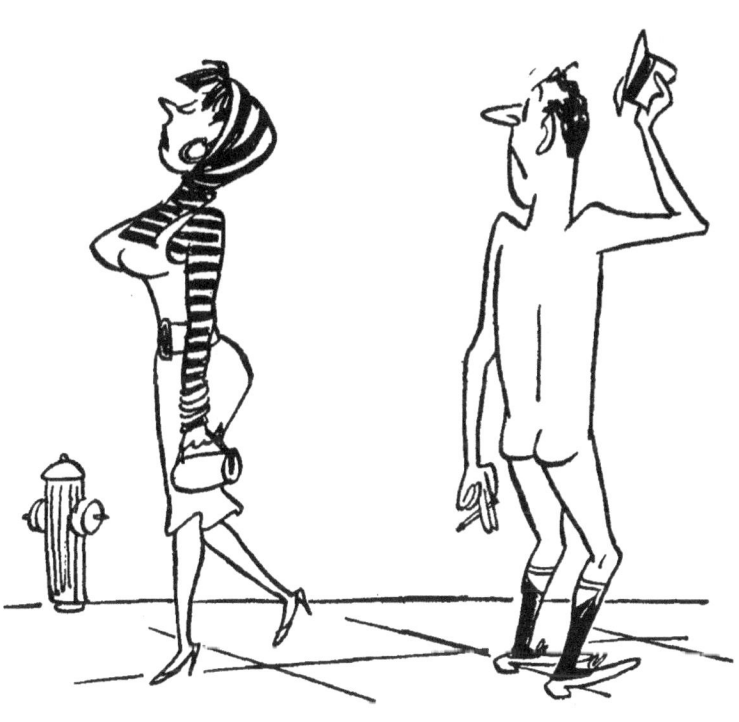

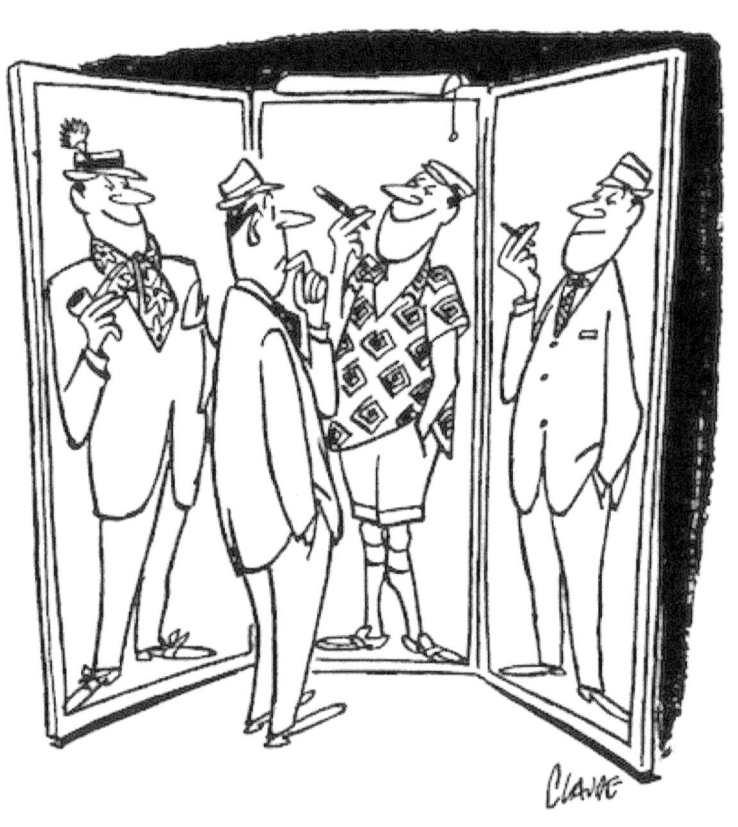

Wear tweeds.

All women like to think they are in the company of intellectuals.

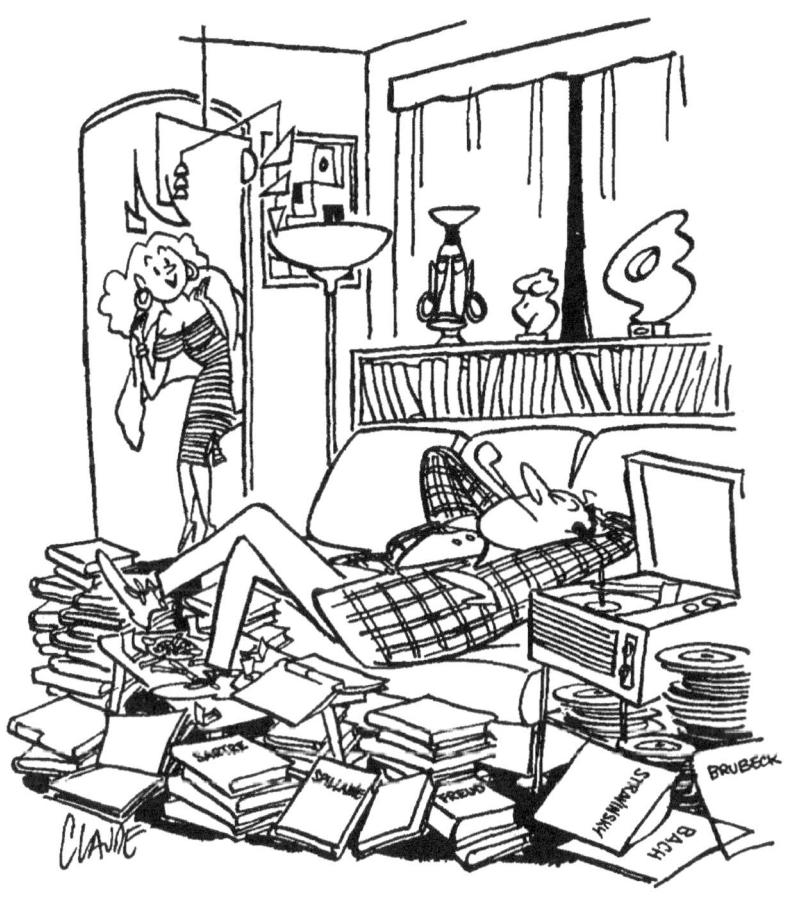

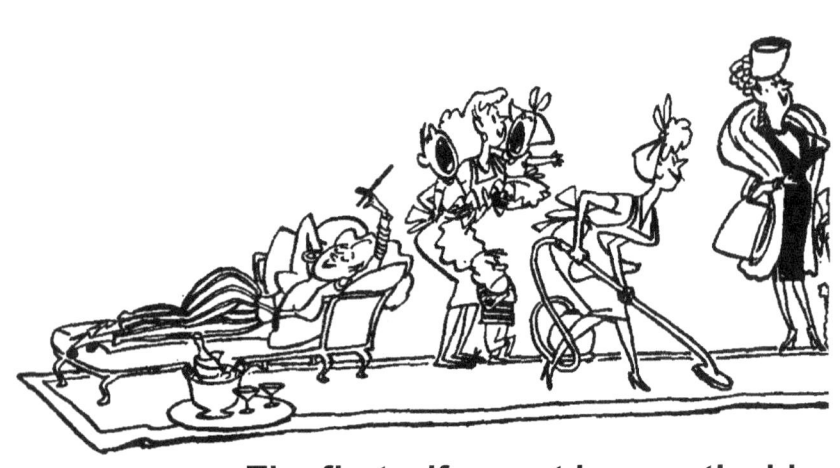

The first wife must be practicable

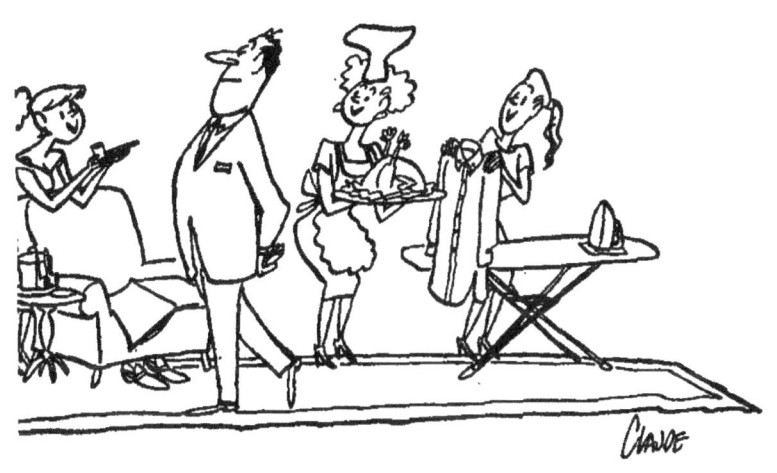

...and serviceable.

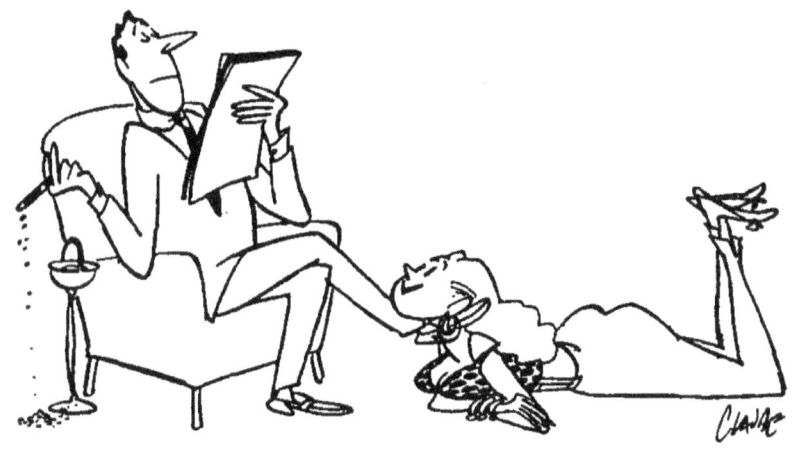

The wife who loves you is hardworking, more efficient.

Just as important is knowing when to kiss.

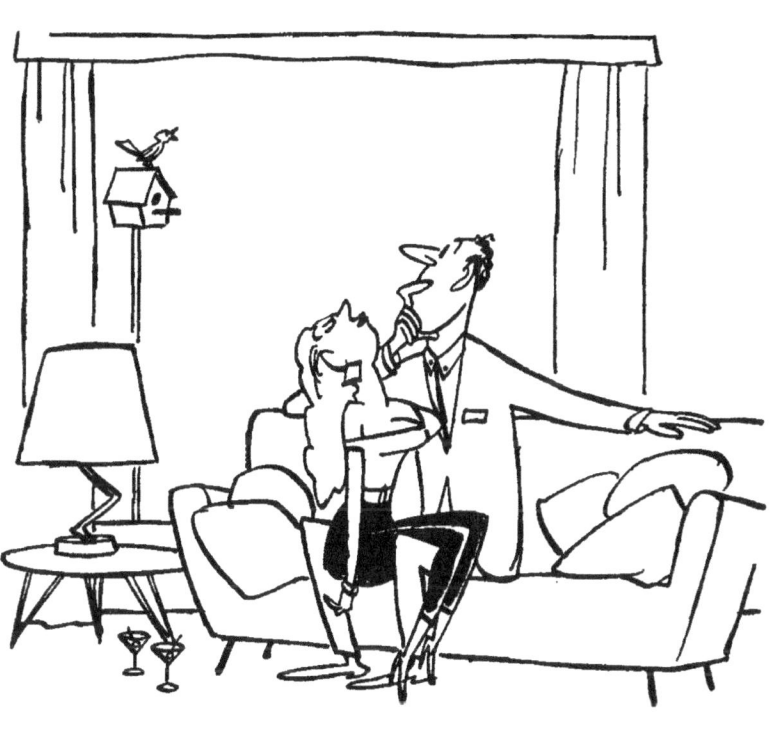

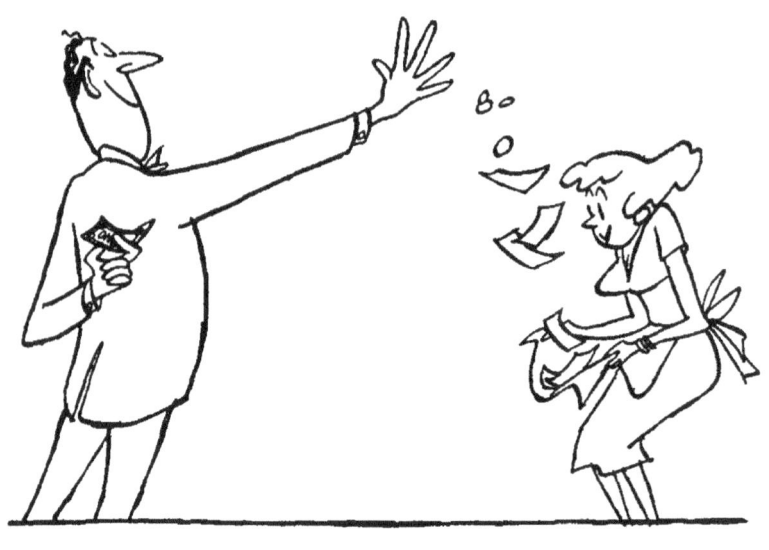

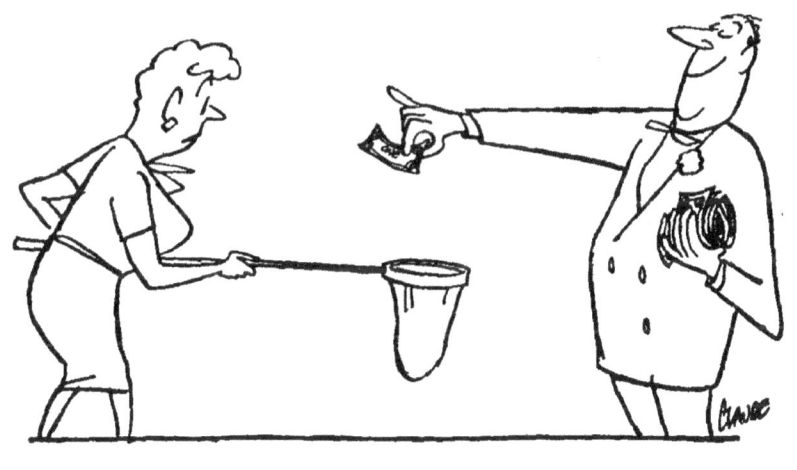

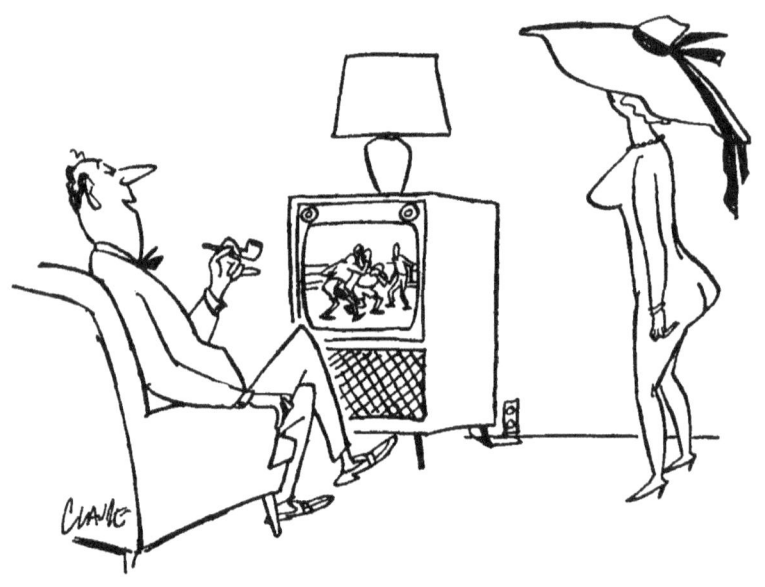

Avoid high style.

The second wife can be chosen differently.

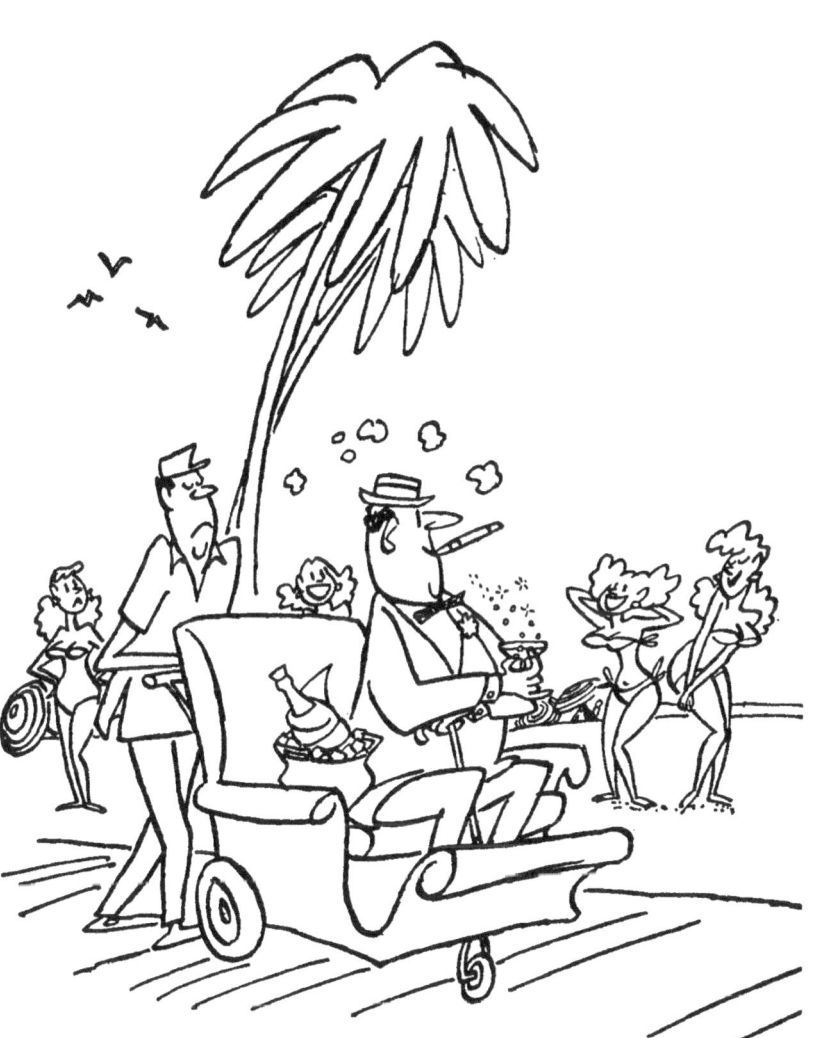

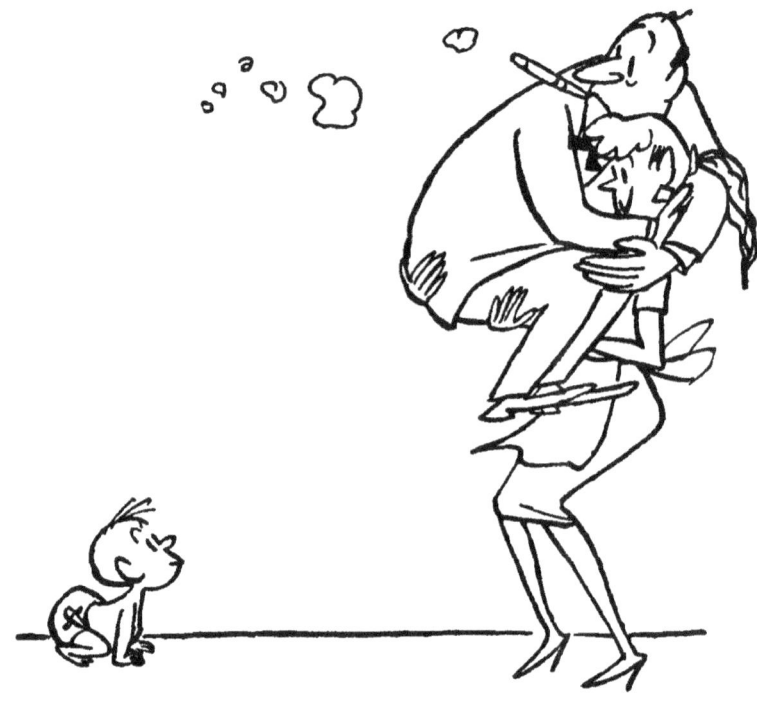

The timid father can miss many happy hours.

It is the man who does the thinking and the woman who does the work.

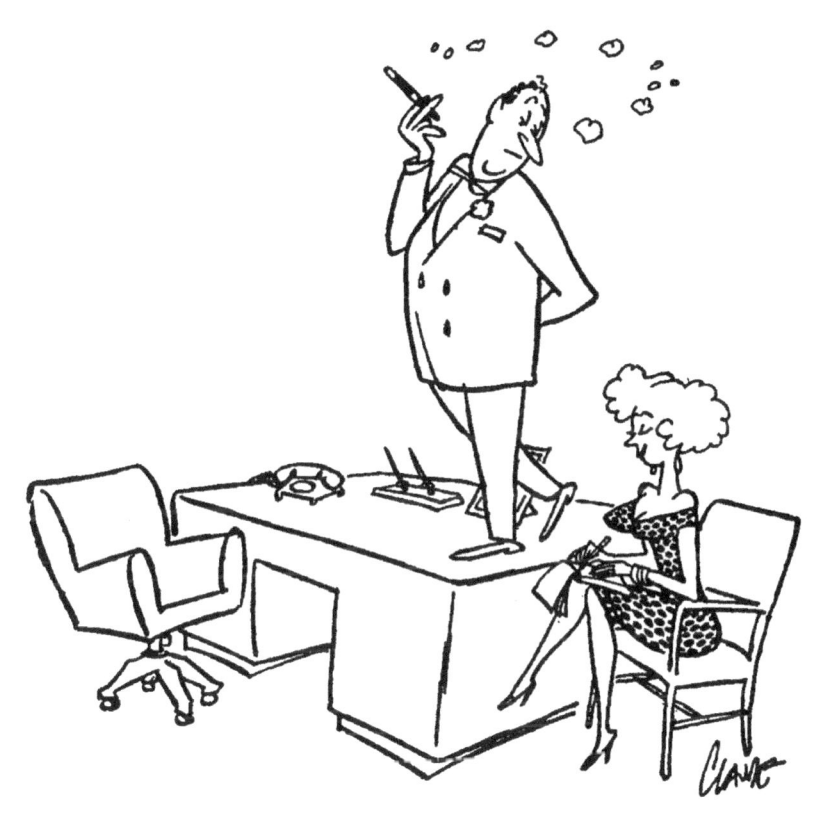